My Kid Can't Spell!

My Kid Can't Spell!

Understanding and Assisting Your Child's Literacy Development

J. Richard Gentry

HEINEMANN
PORTSMOUTH, NH

Heinemann
A division of Reed Elsevier Inc.
361 Hanover Street
Portsmouth, NH 03801-3912

Offices and agents throughout the world

Library of Congress Cataloging-in-Publication Data

Gentry, J. Richard.
My kid can't spell : understanding and assisting your child's
literacy development / J. Richard Gentry.
p. cm.
Includes bibliographical references.
ISBN 0–435–08135–7
1. Spelling ability. 2. English language—Orthography and
spelling—Study and teaching. 3. Reading. 4. Children—Language.
I. Title.
LB1574.G39 1996
372.6'32—dc20   96-25778
                                                                          CIP

EDITOR: Cheryl Kimball
PRODUCTION: Vicki Kasabian
BOOK DESIGN: Jenny Jensen Greenleaf
COVER DESIGN: Michael Leary
MANUFACTURING: Elizabeth Valway

Printed in the United States of America on acid-free paper
99 98 97   DA   2 3 4 5

*This book for parents and teachers
is dedicated with love to*

Bonnie Wright Gentry,

*my mother and my first grade teacher.
She is the first one I remember saying,
"My kid can't spell!"*

Contents

Acknowledgments

This book would not be meaningful without wonderful samples of children's writing collected by parents who share with you the joys and frustrations of their children's spelling development. A special thank you to Eileen Peterson, Eddie and Susan Gentry, Jean and Tim Gillet, Buddy Evans, Carolyn Meigs, and Mitch and Rebekah Pindzola, who made special contributions to this book.

My friend Bill Boswell helped me in my work and gave me guidance and support. Kathy Rogers was my unofficial Atlanta editor who read every word and encouraged me. A special thank you to both of them. Thank you to Cheryl Kimball and Mike Gibbons for their excellent work at Heinemann. Regie Routman, Becky Johnson, and Bill McIntyre gave me their expert professional educator advice. Kent Brown, who publishes marvelous books for children, was gracious and generous in his wisdom. Thanks to Buddy Evans, for convincing me that parents would have interest in what I was writing.

Spelling Right
from the Start

How You Can Help Your Child Take the First Steps as a Reader

If I asked you to make a list of the most important things your child should learn in kindergarten, would you list "spelling"? You should! Spelling opens the gateways to literacy by helping your child meet two requirements for beginning reading:

1. Breaking the code of the alphabet.
2. Learning about sounds in words.

Beyond these two requirements, spelling provides clearly discernible guideposts along your child's journey to literacy. If you know what to look for in his or her spelling, you can monitor your child's progress. Don't be confused. I'm talking about kindergarten and first grade spelling—not the sophisticated dictionary spelling you hope your child will eventually learn. Any serious discussion of spelling should begin with what must happen with kids as spellers in preschool, kindergarten, and first grade.

You may think you didn't start spelling until you were in second grade when you took the spelling book home and memorized words. But if you learned to read in first grade, you already knew a great deal about spelling by the time you got to second grade. In Chapter 2, you will find out how to track your child's literacy development by looking at his or her spelling. But first, let's consider what may happen if your child doesn't learn about spelling right from the start in the journey to literacy.

Learning to Read is Tied to Spelling

Kids break the code that is our alphabet by spelling. They get comfortable with the alphabet and become aware that sounds make up words. These two spelling skills—knowledge of the alphabet and the awareness that sounds make words—actually *predict* success with reading. They are the *only factors known* to be *causally related* to reading achievement! This means they are very important. These skills need to be taught if beginning readers do not have them.

Beyond these first two skills, spelling knowledge continues to support reading development in first grade, where kids need to automatically recognize spelling patterns called "word families." Research suggests that automatic recognition of spelling patterns, such as the ones listed below, enables kids to store words in memory:

The -*at* family: *at–cat–mat–sat*

The -*op* family: *pop–hop–stop–mop*

The -*ake* family: *bake–take–make–rake*

Early learning of these dictionary spellings, along with pattern-to-pattern learning of words, promote reading fluency.

All parents want their children to be reading well by the end of first grade. However, in order for your child to be a successful reader, he or she must also know a lot about spelling. Reading is tied to spelling by the way kids store knowledge about words in memory. The spelling tie to reading is important. Your child's early school experience should include attempts to "invent" spellings, as well as some direct spelling instruction. His or her experience with spelling will provide some of the raw material needed for learning to read.

The most important concept that describes how spelling supports learning to read is that *beginning readers store and retrieve words in memory by letter-sound association.* Letter-sound association is precisely the kind of knowledge being generated when kids invent spellings or learn spelling patterns and word families. What happens in the young reader's mind is more complex than simply sounding out and blending, and certainly much more complex than seeing words as pictures. That's why phonics and whole word explanations for how reading works are often inadequate. These explanations do not account for the complexity of the reading process.

When your young child learns to read, he or she begins to use the letter-sound associations stored in memory by spelling. Simply put, if kids have no experience with spelling, they can't make letter-sound associations—the raw material for reading—in their minds. Remember in grade school when you learned that chlorophyll is the raw material for the complex process of photosynthesis? I suppose you might think of letter-sound associations as the chlorophyll for the complex process of reading!

One Child's Struggle to Break the Alphabet Code

"When I was little I could not read
as good as some people can."
—BLAKE GENTRY, THIRD GRADE

My nephew Blake didn't have the raw material needed for reading in kindergarten and first grade. The story of his personal journey to literacy shows what happens every year to thousands of first grade kids who do not learn about spelling. His story shows why we must not leave kids alone to struggle with breaking the alphabet code or to deal with the rather unnatural process of hearing sounds in words. We can teach these skills by teaching spelling in kindergarten and first grade. Research experts call this "direct instruction in the spelling-to-sound code."

Teaching kindergarten and first grade spelling gives young children the keys to open the gate to early success with reading. It's often said that spelling is a tool for writing. But spelling is much more than that. For emergent literacy, *spelling is a key to reading!* Let's see what happened when Blake *did not* learn about spelling in kindergarten and first grade. Later, in Chapter 2, you will find out what is meant by kindergarten and first grade spelling, and what needs to be taught.

There was nothing wrong when Blake entered kindergarten. He was healthy, attractive, intelligent, and well adjusted. He loved books and enjoyed being read to. Whenever I visited my nephew, Blake begged me to read some of our favorite books.

"Did you bring the wolf book?" he would ask, insisting on hearing Jon Scieszka's *The True Story of the Three Little Pigs* for the fiftieth time. I finally gave him his own copy.

Undaunted by the prospect of learning to read, write, and spell, Blake was preoccupied with activities on the farm, dinosaurs, and driving the tractor—which he talked about incessantly. He was a perfectly normal budding kindergartner.

That first year of school, I noticed Blake doing little reading and writing—and no spelling. His kindergarten in North Carolina followed a curriculum called "Circle of Childhood." It focused on socialization and building self-worth.

(Hundreds of school districts across North America follow similar curricula.) As I pondered Blake's kindergarten experience, I remembered having read an account of another North Carolina kindergarten child: "The year 1947 found me in North Carolina where I entered kindergarten and learned to play and socialize better than I had," Mary Burkhardt had written a number of years before in the foreword of Rudolf Flesch's *Why Johnny Still Can't Read.* "Reading was not allowed." It was disconcerting to wonder if kindergartens could still be places where reading, writing, and spelling were not allowed!

One year later, Blake entered first grade. His teachers were still dutifully following the "Circle of Childhood" curriculum. I was surprised to learn, in September of his first grade year, that Blake did not know the letters of the alphabet or the sounds in words. It surprised me that he was not inventing spellings. Although he enjoyed books, he had not broken the alphabet code or related spelling to sound and meaning.

I knew that breaking the code, or learning about spelling in kindergarten, was one small part of the larger task of learning to read. In addition, kids need to be read to, and to share in the reading of storybooks. They need to be immersed in both reading and writing from the very beginning because reading and writing focus on getting meaning from print. Breaking the code is a necessary but not sufficient condition for developing good reading comprehension ability.

I was worried because I knew Blake had a serious problem. As a professor of elementary education and reading, I have worked for twenty years with hundreds of beginning readers—kids just like Blake. In that time, largely due to new developments in research, many teachers and researchers have reached new levels of understanding about the importance of spelling to emergent literacy. During that same time, I had become recognized as a national expert on teaching spelling. My spelling research, spelling text-books, books on spelling for teachers, and work on the educational speaking circuit had taken me across North America, South America, Europe, and Australia to talk with teachers and parents about spelling. It was especially pain-ful for a national spokesperson on spelling to watch his nephew, who was perfectly capable, fail to learn about spelling in kindergarten and first grade!

Blake's problem was not developmental. Certainly I was aware that children's literacy develops at different paces. Developmental aspects do come into play when kids learn to read. But I knew Blake *was* developmentally ready. Readiness alone is not enough. The alphabet and aware-ness of sounds in words must be learned. Information about the alphabet and sounds must be put in front of children so that kids can bump into it! This was not happening for Blake—at home or at school. I knew that Blake's missing knowledge about the alphabet and how sounds make words would make learning to read very difficult under any cir-cumstances.

By December of his first grade year, Blake was strug-gling. He had an intense desire to read and write, but he couldn't invent spellings. He dictated a letter to his mother and meticulously copied it, making sure every word was perfectly spelled:

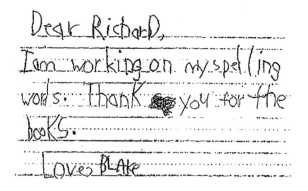

Had Blake received appropriate spelling instruction, he would have known more about the alphabet, inventing spellings, and sounds and patterns in words. Without such instruction, Blake lacked the raw material for reading, even though he had been developmentally ready for a very long time. Without it, he couldn't write on his own. He was immensely puzzled by the alphabet code, but no one showed him how it worked! When I visited in December, I found that Blake *still* did not know some of the letters of the alphabet. He was even more confused about how sounds worked in words.

There was other bad news. Blake was beginning to not like school. He said to me in December, "I think I'm stupid, Uncle Richard" and "I don't like reading."

In January, Blake's mother went to his school for a parent-teacher conference. She learned from the teacher what I already knew. "Yes," the teacher reported, "Blake is having problems."

Blake struggled with reading through the remaining months of first grade. By the end of the year, he was at least half a year behind. He passed first grade, but he felt like a failure.

The "Circle of Childhood" experience, designed to pump up Blake's self-worth during his kindergarten year, did not work. Blake's self-esteem was at the lowest point in his life. By *not* teaching "kindergarten spelling," which would have helped Blake break the alphabet code, the curriculum failed him. "Circle of Childhood" did not release the real self-esteem that surely would have developed had Blake learned to read and write. I'm afraid it undermined Blake's real kindergarten education: learning the letters of the alphabet; learning about sounds and spelling; exploring paper and pencil activity; taking the first steps in becoming a reader and writer; and enjoying nursery rhymes, poems, and good children's literature. None of these received appropriate focus.

After kindergarten and a year in first grade, Blake was a "failure" at reading and writing. He was crushed, ashamed, and devastated. Unfortunately, no one had helped him take the first steps on the journey to literacy.

Your Can Help

As a parent, *you* can help your child take those first steps as a reader and writer. Here are some guidelines you may wish to follow. Which of the listed activities are you presently engaged in? Which might be ways to provide your emergent reader with further support? Notice the prominence of spelling. We have failed to teach spelling—both at school and at home—in the past. Supporting your emergent reader as a speller is one important way to ensure that he or she learns to read well by the end of first grade.

Guidelines for Parents of an Emergent Reader

- ❏ Read and enjoy storybooks on a regular basis with your child.
- ❏ Read and enjoy lots of alphabet books with your child.
- ❏ Read and enjoy nursery rhymes, poetry, and lots of books with rhyming words and rhyming patterns, because the experience of word play and hearing different sounds in words is helpful for beginning readers.
- ❏ When reading aloud to your child, make reading fun because enjoying books turns kids into readers.
- ❏ Recognize that literacy emerges at different paces for different children.
- ❏ Encourage and try to help your child to learn the names and shapes of the letters of the alphabet.
- ❏ Recognize that spelling and writing and reading happen in tandem—not in a serial, lockstep fashion.

❏ Recognize that invented spelling predicts reading achievement, and for this reason, encourage it.

❏ Whenever your emergent reader wants to communicate in writing, say, "That's great!"

❏ Say "Spell it like it sounds" or "Spell it like you think it looks" or "Try it on your own" and then explain, "You aren't supposed to know all the dictionary spellings yet."

❏ Sometimes spell the word for your child and praise him or her for writing it.

❏ Be sensible about invented spellings and do not expect your first grader to spell like an adult.

❏ Learn more about invented spelling so that you can monitor your child's literacy development.

❏ Recognize that invented spelling is tied to reading by the way kids store words in memory—not through sounding out and blending (phonics).

❏ Recognize that reading is much more complex than sounding out and blending, so you will not be obsessed with phonics.

❏ Recognize that teachers who teach spelling *are* teaching phonics.

❏ Do not be obsessed with phonics! (I include this item twice because so many parents make this mistake.)

❏ Expect your child's school experience to include some direct spelling instruction in kindergarten and first grade.

❏ Remain upbeat and supportive, and try to maintain a positive attitude about your child's literacy development.

❏ Try to be supportive of your child's teachers and of your child's school.

These guidelines will open gates, provide guide-posts, and help get your child off to a good start on the journey to literacy.

I am pleased to report that Blake is on a happier journey. He is now both a reader and a writer. In the summer after his first grade year, his parents hired a tutor who plugged up the holes in Blake's kindergarten and first grade education. In essence, his tutor taught him kindergarten and first grade spelling. Many of the suggestions in the checklist were followed.

We are proud of Blake's success. When I went to North Carolina for a visit in July after Blake's second grade year, I found one of his stories attached to the refrigerator door with a magnet. The story validates Blake as a reader and a writer. It is bursting with affirmation of his wisdom and self-worth. I offer it here—copied so you can easily read it. Then I share it in the version he wrote so you can enjoy his writing of it, his spelling, and his art.

Dive Into a Book
By Blake Gentry

Did you know that when you read a book it helps your brain? When I was little I could not read as good as some people can. But it all came to me. So the next time you get a book, do not quit reading it. Get your mother or father to hear you read. If you get a book and can't read it, just try. Go to the library and read a book. Books are fun to read in. Some people don't read, they watch TV all the time. Stories are fun to do. Don't watch TV. It is bad for your brain. If you do watch TV, read a book. Some books might be too hard for you to read. Get a book that you can read. Big kids get big books. Little kids get little books. When school is out read every day and make your brain smart. Read and read. Don't watch TV. IT'S COOL TO READ!

by Blake Gentry

Dive into a Book

Did you know that When you read a Book it helps your Brain? When I was Little i could not read as good as Some People can. But it all came to me. So the Next Time you get a Book Do not Quiet reading, it. Get your mother or Fathe to here you read, If you get a Book and can't read it Just trai. go to the Libore and read a Book. Books are fun to read in. Some People Don't read they Waich tv all the time. Storys are fun to Do. Don't Waich tv it is Bad for your Brain. If you Do waich tv read a Book. Some Books might Be to hard for you to Read. Get a Book that you can read. Big kids get Big Books. Litte kids get Little Books. When school is out read even Day and make our Brain smart. read and read. Don't Waich tv.

The End

COOl Book! It's cool to read!

2

Is Your Kindergartner or First Grader Developmentally on Track?

Checking the Developmental Guideposts

Spelling provides an easy check on your child's level of literacy development. If you know the developmental guideposts to look for, it's one of the easiest ways to monitor a child's progress. Keep in mind that language development—speaking, reading, and writing—does not happen at the same time for all children. But the five spelling stages presented in this chapter will give you a good *general* indication of your child's level of development.

Educators often use the terms "invented spelling," "developmental spelling," and "temporary spelling" to describe the stages of spelling you will see in this chapter. The term "invented" actually comes from the work of the psychologist Jean Piaget, whose theories explain how children go about "reinventing" language. Given appropriate exposure and experiences with print in natural language contexts, each child actually "invents" or "reinvents" spelling in stages.

Actually, you have already experienced developmental stages if you watched your child's development of speech.

You may recall a babbling stage, a stage when the first words were spoken, and even a stage when ideas were expressed in just two words like "all-gone milk." Eventually your child spoke language just like you do. Spelling likewise develops in stages. In this chapter, you will explore five developmental stages of spelling and learn how to identify them. You will find out when they occur, and what they show about your child's literacy development.

If your child is in kindergarten, look for Stage 1 spelling: *Experimenting with writing and the alphabet.*

Five-year-old Dan and his mom are on the way to the grocery store. Dan pulls out his notepad and crayon and makes a grocery list. Can you read it?

You probably guessed "7-Up"; maybe "eggs" and "fish"; and perhaps "mousse"—like the styling mousse Dan might use on his hair.

When Dan's mother asked him to tell her what was on his grocery list, he replied, "7-Up, bran flakes, milk, doughnuts." His spelling doesn't even look close to the words he was thinking about!

Recognizing environmental print like "7-Up" and inventing the grocery list spellings—

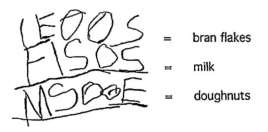

—is remarkable and quite good for five-year-old Dan. Even though his first invented spellings are strings of random letters that you can't possibly read, this is a natural beginning for a speller. Speakers begin by babbling sounds; spellers begin by "babbling" letters.

Two important things are happening in this example of Stage 1 spelling. First, Dan is discovering the *function* of writing. The function in this case is a grocery list. Functional or purposeful writing is its own reinforcement for literacy development. Do not worry that the *form* is not yet perfect. It is not supposed to be! As when Dan learned to speak, the function of his language must come *before* perfect form. The idea that function comes before form is a basic principle of language learning.

Second, Dan's Stage 1 spelling provides an opportunity for learning. He is rehearsing and expanding his knowledge of the alphabet. He is taking risks and making hypotheses about how spelling works. Inventing spellings allows Dan to *think* about spelling and its relationship to the whole scheme of printed language, writing, and reading.

Many kids actually break the alphabet code when they experiment with invented spelling. By experimenting with writing, they break the code that helps them learn to read. It is widely recognized among educators that some kids write first and read later. Stage 1 spelling, then, should always be valued and encouraged in kindergarten.

Even though you cannot read Stage 1 spelling such as Dan's grocery list, it is powerful diagnostically. In fact, it is a window into the mind of the writer that allows you to see how the writer is thinking about print. You can see, for example, that at this stage of writing, Dan did not know many letters of the alphabet (notice his overuse of *o, e,* and *s*). In addition, he did not know that letters stand for sounds.

While Stage 1 spelling is a signal of positive development in five-year-old Dan, it would not be a good sign for a writer at the beginning of first grade. The Stage 1 speller's limited knowledge of the alphabet and of how sounds work in words would likely make learning to read very complicated. As we saw in Chapter 1, knowledge of the alphabet and the ability to segment the sounds in words are predictors of success with reading in first grade. It is desirable, then, for kids to start the year with some foundation in this knowledge. If they are only Stage 1 spellers, they do not yet have these important tools for constructing a foundation for reading.

At the end of kindergarten and the beginning of first grade, look for Stage 2 spelling: *Demonstrating phonemic awareness.*

It's near the end of kindergarten year and Dan brings home a piece of writing that looks like this:

"This is great! What does it say?" Dan's mom asks enthusiastically.

"Well," Dan explains, "It's about last weekend when I went to Brad's house and we had a birthday party and it was fun to play with Richie."

Since Dan wrote the piece earlier that day in school, he may not be sure of the exact wording of the story. But his mom makes a powerful discovery. She recognizes some words in the story by their spelling.

BHS	=	*Brad's house*
PRT	=	*party*
BTDA	=	b*irth*day

Dan is moving from Stage 1 to Stage 2 spelling. He is beginning to represent sounds in some words in his writing, and his mom can recognize some of Dan's words even though the spellings are very abbreviated.

This spelling is a giant step in development. It is like the cognitive leap Dan made when he moved from babbling to using his first spoken words. Only here the leap is from random letter spellings to spellings that represent sounds.

Dan is demonstrating more control of the alphabet, and for the first time in his writing he is using letters to represent sounds. Educators would say he is demonstrating "phonemic awareness."

Phonemic awareness is the ability to segment the speech sounds in words. For example, if I asked you to say the sounds you hear in the word "rat," you might say /r/ – /a/– /t/. If I asked you to clap one time for each sound and you clapped three times, you would be demonstrating phonemic awareness. Dan is demonstrating the beginnings of phonemic awareness when he writes BHS for *Brad's house* and BTDA for *birthday*. He is taking a giant step along the path to literacy.

In the middle of first grade, look for Stage 3 spelling: *Spelling words by ear.*

If your child is a first grader, you can enjoy looking for a fascinating stage when kids invent spellings almost exclusively by ear. With first graders who are developmentally on track, it often appears between October and the end of February. By this time, many first graders have become familiar with the alphabet, have had practice stretching out the sounds in words, and have become familiar with writing invented spellings. Stage 3 spellers focus on what they hear. For example, they use letter names to spell words, as in A-T-E- for *eighty*. If you say *eighty* slowly and stretch out the /E/ sound at the end of the word, you hear the Stage 3 spelling. This gives you an idea of how your child is thinking about spelling at Stage 3.

Look at these samples of Stage 3 spelling. Can you read them?

TO A ME
PLES
TO COM
M ICOM
PRT

The three Pig's
Lillte
one bay a Mut
hr. PiG SeNt.
her three Lillte
PiG's Ot iNot
The WoD's.
The Frst LitL PiG
Met a MaN Wit
a BuN Dl. uV.
CtRo

The PiG SeI
tAte
MaN GiV m
CtoR to ﮩ BilD my
hus

Even though many of the spellings in these samples do not look like English spelling, you probably can read them with very little difficulty.

To Amy,
Please come to my party.

The Three Little Pigs

One day a mother pig sent her three little pigs out into the woods. The first little pig met a man with a bundle of straw.

The pig said to the man, "Give me straw to build my house."

Spelling by ear is much more complex than it may appear. This level of spelling has been thoroughly researched; findings indicate that children's categorizations of speech sounds and their invented spellings at this level are ingenious, complex, systematic, and perceptually accurate.

Parents often worry that children will become locked into this stage, or that writing misspelled words will be harmful. Actually, writing and inventing spelling in this manner is the very best way to get the beginner to *think* about spelling. Stage 3 spelling promotes new learning.

In first grade, spelling by ear is as natural for the speller as saying "all-gone milk" or "daddy bye-bye" is for the two-year-old speaker. You do not expect your two-year-old to say "My father has departed"! Two-year-old kids don't speak like adults! First graders won't *spell* like adults either. The more your first grader enjoys writing and inventing spelling, the more he or she is learning. The function of writing comes long before perfect form. Your child has plenty of time ahead to become an expert speller.

As the parent of a first grader, you should celebrate Stage 3 spelling. At Stage 3, kids can write anything they can say, and you will have great fun reading it.

At the end of first grade and in second grade, look for Stage 4 spelling: *Spelling words by eye.*

Kids who are moving along the developmentally appropriate path are generally learning to read in first grade. Their brains are being bombarded with visual images of print. Children look at the print in books every day in school—probably much more than at any previous time in their lives. This new focus on the visual images of printed English and increased time-on-task reading and writing has a powerful impact on spelling. It will cause your child to take another giant cognitive leap, this one into Stage 4 spelling. Instead of spelling words like he or she *hears* them, your child will begin to spell words like he or she *sees* them. ATE (*eighty*), for example, might become EIGHTEE. OPN (*open* spelled by ear) might become OPIN (*open* spelled by eye). Sometimes spelling by eye results in unusual-looking spellings, like YOUNIGHTED STAYTS for *United States*. This is actually a pretty sophisticated spelling, based on visual patterns often seen in text. A young speller may not have seen the word *united* very often because it appears infrequently in text, but they will have seen *you* and *night* and the ending *-ed*. Since Stage 4 spellers are just beginning to use the visual strategy, their knowledge of visually inspired patterns is not fully integrated, resulting in very unusual spellings.

Along with unusual, visually influenced spellings, you may notice many more words being spelled conventionally. Look at second grader Amber's sample of Stage 4 spelling:

Good THING to Eat

I like STRALBARES and I like ORRANGE
I like tomato SUPE and I like PECHIS.
I like apples and I like BROCULE.
I like COLEFALWORE TO, you know.
I like corn and I like green BENES.
I like FRIDE CHEKEN and I like BARBO Q Cheken
But most of all I like HO MAED SPOGATE.
THOSS [Those] things are good for you.
That why I put them down.

Did you notice how many of Amber's invented spellings are influenced by the visual conventions of English spelling?

SUPE (*soup*)	*Vowel–consonant–silent e* is a high-frequency visual pattern.
PECHIS (*peaches*)	Using vowels in every syllable, Amber spells PECHIS by eye, not by ear, which would be PECHS.
BENES (*beans*)	*Vowel-consonant-silent e* is a high-frequency visual pattern.
FRIDE (*fried*)	If *ride* is *r-i-d-e*, why not *f-r-i-d-e* for *fried?*
MAED (*made*)	*A* and *E* are seen together in words like *Mae*, so MAED looks good for *made*.
TO (*too*)	*To* is the most frequently used and viewed of the words *to, too,* and *two.*
COLEFLAWORE (*cauliflower*)	COL-E-FLA-WORE is a perfectly good visual spelling for the syllables in *cauliflower.*

Stage 4 is one of the most important stages for teachers to look for. It is a signal that children are ready for more formal study of the patterns and consistency of English spelling. Here are some of the visual patterns you will see in your child's Stage 4 spelling.

- vowels in every syllable
- visual patterns, such as *vowel-consonant-silent e* in the long vowel spellings *-ake, -eke, -ike, -oke,* and *-uke*
- the visual convention of pairing vowels, such as *ae, ai, ee, ea, ie, ei, oo, ou,* and *ui*
- the visual convention of coupling letters, such as *ll, rr, ss, mm,* and *nn*

When you see lots of these visually inspired spellings, it's time for your child to benefit from more formal spelling instruction. Traditionally, such instruction has begun in grade two. That's exactly when many kids start using Stage 4 spelling. It happens developmentally. So look for Stage 4 spelling as a signal for more formal spelling instruction in school.

In the next chapter, we will look at how conventional spelling develops (Stage 5), and at which words and patterns kids should master at each grade level. But first, here are some tips and strategies for helping your child progress through the first four stages.

Some General Guidelines, Tips, and Strategies for Early Spelling Stages

STAGE 1 SPELLING
- ❑ Read aloud and share children's books.
- ❑ Encourage paper and pencil activity, writing, and experimenting with the alphabet.
- ❑ Share alphabet books.
- ❑ Model writing and allow kids to send greeting cards, make grocery lists, or just pretend to write.
- ❑ Whenever you are writing, call it to your child's attention—talk about what you are writing.

STAGE 2 SPELLING

❏ Read nursery rhymes, poems, familiar stories, and other good children's literature.
❏ Play lots of games with sounds and rhyming words using strategies like these:

> What word would be left if the /K/ sound were taken away from *cat?*
> Do *pig* and *pipe* begin with the same sound?
> What word would you have if you put these sounds together: /s/-/a/-/t/ (*sat*)
> What sounds do you hear in *rat?*
> How many sounds do you hear in *cake?* (three: /k/ /a/ /k/)
> Which word starts with a different sound: *bag, nine, beach, bike?*
> Is there a /k/ in *bike?* (yes)

> (Adapted from Keith E. Stanovich, "Romance and Reality," *The Reading Teacher*, January 1994, 283.)

STAGE 3 SPELLING

❏ Encourage purposeful writing.
❏ Give lots of praise.
❏ Say things like "Hey, that's pretty good spelling for a first grader!"; "I like the way you figured out how to spell it by ear"; and "I'll help you look it up in the dictionary. See, here's how it looks. You'll soon be spelling it this way all by yourself!"
❏ If you are a lousy speller, say "I've always been a lousy speller! If you keep making progress, I may soon be coming to you for help!"

STAGE 4 SPELLING

❏ Continue to encourage purposeful writing and give lots of praise.
❏ Notice that many words in your child's writing (about half or more) are spelled correctly.

❏ Occasionally ask your child to circle one or two words in a story that he or she wasn't sure how to spell. Ask the child to "have a go" at the correct spelling. After the child gives it their best shot, help "hunt down" the correct spelling by looking it up in the dictionary.

❏ Encourage your child to become a "word hunter" by forming a habit of consciously looking for the words that he or she needs to know how to spell. Help your child keep a list of "Words I Need to Know How To Spell When I Write."

❏ Encourage your child to learn to spell a few unknown words each week.

❏ If your child is in at least second grade and is a Stage 4 speller, he or she needs some focus on spelling in school. Look for four spelling-related activities each week in school:

1. Finding unknown words to spell (about ten each week).
2. Inspecting word patterns.
3. Mastering new spellings.
4. Connecting spelling with writing.

If these activities aren't occurring, find out why!

Favorite Samples: Kids Finding Their Voices

Kids have been sharing samples of their spelling with me for years. Here are some of my favorites, written in invented spelling. These pieces will help you know what to look for from the budding writer at your house. When I read these pieces I don't so much notice the spelling as hear the writer's voice. Some of these pieces are timeless and priceless—as will be your son or daughter's invented spelling. For a moment, let's not worry so much about the mechanics, the process, and the complexity of spelling. Please read these just for enjoyment.

Let each piece help you put spelling in the proper perspective and into its appropriate context. Here are my favorites.

Jean and Tim Gillet's daughter, Leslie, has charmed thousands of readers with her spelling which was reported in the book Jean and I co-authored, *Teaching Kids to Spell* (Heinemann, 1993).

Description of a Flock of Butterflies, Leslie Gillet—Prekindergarten
(a Stage 1 speller)

"Humpty Dumpty," Leslie Gillet—Kindergarten
(a Stage 2 speller)

"My Motor Boat," Michael Pindzola—Kindergarten
(a Stage 2 speller)

Michael Pindzola captured a moment of exhilaration—Kindergarten
(a Stage 3 speller)

My Babe store

I was baon on
Janurre the 4. I
Git baon At 5-o-lo
I Wool Aras 1 Pant.
ThE farst time I
weat to Weastn saln
I dead a skxee in
my Moms Lap. I
War a wiet dras
Neth Las on est.

And at had ABCs
on at. I ate ham
Ahd Grren Bers meat.
Meredith Ann
Edwards

Meredith Ann Edwards wrote "My Baby Story" in kindergarten. She grew up to be a cheerleader and honor student at Wake Forest University.
(a Stage 3 speller)

Published in my book *Spel...Is a Four-Letter Word* (Heinemann, 1987)

My feet.
are flesh.
I whair
sis 3.
My feet take
me evrewhair.
My feet like
to clime trees
and billdings,
I walk to
School.
My feet
make me
Swem in
water. My
feet are
tiyerd at
the end
of the
day

My foot

Dan Meigs wrote this wonderful piece in first grade. He is now an honor student at the University of North Carolina at Chapel Hill.
(a Stage 4 speller)

Published in my book *Spel...Is a Four-Letter Word* (Heinemann, 1987)

Thing Kids look for in Teachers
1. Kids are treated equal regardless of rase color etc
2. do alot of hand on projets with kids
3. can be seen clerly by every kid
4. ponish only kid whos a problen not whole class
5. try to stay down of writing rones on board
6. not known to pattel
7. decorate room for holoday let kids help
8. have a clock that everyone can see
9. have a calander of events and the date
10. dacorat desk walls and even seling
11. not to nice and not to mean
12. share thing with class
13. try not to have assand seats
14. be abel to see everyone from Desk
15. keep extra paper and pencels hadey
16. try to ware difrent clotes every day
17. keep enciklopitys and dictiory hadey
18. try not to have sobscitutes
19. have a globe
20. try not to give homecwork on friday
21. exsplane thing untel kid undrstand
22. have alot of book to read
23. have plant in room
24. give little gefts on specal holodays
25. try to have a small, live anenils like gerbel of hernet chacbdbs

Noah Miller wrote this priceless list of "Things Kids Look for in Teachers" for his mother, Robin Minnick, when she received her teaching degree. I have shared it with thousands of teachers across North America.

Dear Uncle Richard,

Thank you so much for the trip to Atlanta. I'm very lucky to have you as my uncle. You do a lot for me and I appreciate the things you do.

You and Carol are fun to be around. You guy's thought of great places to go like the Swan House and UNDER GROUND. I loved that one—you know—where we ate Mexican food and Carol told the waiter he was SEXEST. I learned a lot from Carol, but don't worry.

Well, I started school. Math is not my subject. BOC [block] Studies is. My teacher is great. Her name is Miss Hubbard. She has this way of teaching you. I make all A's in her class.

Well, got to go. See YA at the dinner table for turkey and stuffing.

Love,
Stacy G.

P.S. I want long hair! I had to say SONTHING NAGITIVE. My TOUNG would have FALLEN out. BUY.

Stacy Gentry's great-grandmother, Rosa, could spell every word in the dictionary. (I know, I personally asked her how to spell most of them.) Stacy's mother is a super speller. Stacy will likely be a lousy speller the rest of her life—just like her Uncle Richard.

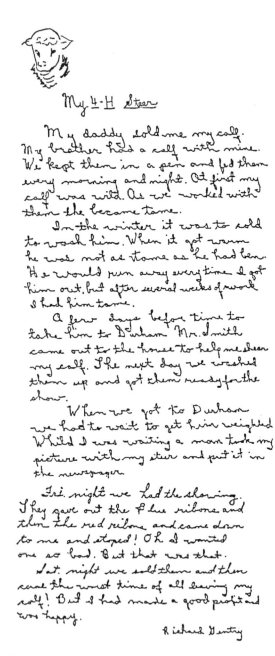

My 4-H Steer

My daddy sold me my calf. My brother had a calf with mine. We kept them in a pen and fed them every morning and night. At first my calf was wild. As we worked with them the became tame.

In the winter it was to cold to wash him. When it got warm he was not as tame as he had ben. He would run away everytime I got him out, but after several weeks of work I had him tame.

A few days before time to take him to Durham Mr. Smith came out to the house to help me shear my calf. The next day we washed them up and got them ready for the show.

When we got to Durham we had to wait to get him weighed Whild I was waiting a man took my picture with my steer and put it in the newspaper.

Fri. night we had the showing. They gave out the flue ribons and then the red ribon and came down to me and stoped! Oh I wanted one so bad. But that was that.

Sat. night we sold them and then came the worst time of all leaving my calf! But I had made a good profit and was happy.

Richard Gentry

I struggled with spelling over three decades ago, when I was a fifth grader. Had my teachers understood what to look for, they could have helped me better prepare for my lifelong difficulty with expert spelling. The mistakes in this piece—THE for *they*, BEN for *been*, WHILD for *while*, STOPED for *stopped*, and RIBONS for *ribbons*—all indicate my brain's difficulty with storing and retrieving the visual forms of words. Somehow I made it as a writer, but at times I still can't spell *before*.

Dear uncle Richard

The farm is doing great for me and Grannd Mother. I have a dog and a cat the cat came from the wild It is a male cat and adult cat he is very Smart. The dog is not so happy with the cat he is sad because I do not pay much atenchen to him. I am older now and stronger than a 80 pound Boy and smarter. P.S. Say hay to Bill for me. write to me some time Please?!!!

Love Stacy and Blake

Blake Gentry wrote this coming-of-age piece at the beginning of third grade. I like the changes he sees in himself. "I am older now and stronger than an 80 pound boy, and smarter." (a Stage 3 speller)

How Well Does Your Child in Second Through Eighth Grade Spell?

Looking for Stage 5: Conventional Spelling

> "We like to hit the hockey PUKE."
> Michael Pindzola, *First Grade*

By now you may be thinking, "Enough of this invented spelling! When is my child going to start spelling correctly?" The answer is—you must be patient. Expert spelling is not easy, and, for many children, it is not as natural as learning to speak. Conventional spelling is learned over a long period of time. Typically, most kids will need to study the patterns and consistency of English spelling for about seven years—from grade two through grade eight—before they can spell like adults.

Here's the other bad news: About one in five kids may *never* become expert spellers. In Chapter 5 we will learn why some kids and adults struggle with expert spelling all of their lives.

Look at this sample, "My Miserable Week of School Vacation," which Jason wrote when he was in second grade. You will enjoy reading it.

My Miserebull Week of
Schooll Vacashon
lost week It was Schooll
Vacashon it was miserebill
the thersday ∧ nite befor
vacashon my sister let out
a blud cerdeling skream
mom ran into myn and my
sisters room and smakt her
foot on the byuro
and was on kruchis
we coldent go
rolerskating or bolling or
enething it was borring
and on-top of that
my sister was driving me
crasi. and by the time
friday came i was fed
up with avrething. saterday
morning I had Karata
edlest a chang of
senirey

After you have read Jason's piece, look at it again, but this time pay particular attention to his spelling.

Now it's time to pop the big question: Is Jason a good speller or a poor speller?

Many parents would look at this piece and be horrified by the spelling. Actually, Jason is an excellent writer and a good speller for a second grader.

About one-third of the words in Jason's piece are misspelled. How, you may ask, can Jason be a *good* speller?

Remember, very young children, even second graders like Jason, are not supposed to spell like adults. Jason's spelling is developmentally on track. Most of his misspelled words are words that second graders are not supposed to be able to spell. His invented spellings, however, show that he is thinking about spelling in ways appropriate for his age and stage of development.

Jason is very much into Stage 4 spelling. He is spelling by eye, which demonstrates the very positive practice of inventing spellings with visually inspired patterns. Here are some examples:

SCHOOLL	*School* is a third grade level word—that is to say, by the end of second grade, most kids can't spell it, but by the end of third grade, most kids can. Jason has recalled the double *o*'s in school and he has noticed double *l*'s at the end of many English words, so he tries OO and LL in SCHOOLL.
THERSDAY	*Thursday* is a fifth grade level word. Jason hasn't studied spellings for the days of the week and he hasn't learned the rule for capitalizing them. In most curricula, the rule for capitalizing days of the week is taught in third grade.
NITE	*Night* is a third grade level word. Jason should be exposed to different spellings of the long *i* sound when he studies spelling patterns

for long vowel sounds in grades
two and three.

BORRING   *Boring* is a fourth grade level
word. The rule about doubling the
consonant before an ending
likewise is a higher level skill most
often taught at the end of second
grade or in third grade. But Jason
has already noticed from visual
inspection of print that *R* is often
doubled in words before -*ing* is
added, so he tries it here.

Jason relied on visual aspects of English spelling to
invent spellings for twenty words in this Stage 4 piece:

MISEREBULL	NITE	SISTERS	ENETHING
SCHOOLL	BEFOR	BYURO	BORRING
VACASHON	CERDELING	KRUCHIS	ON-TOP
MISEREBILL	SKREAM	ROLERSKATING	SATERDAY
THERSDAY	MYN	BOLLING	SENIREY

These are difficult words for a second grade speller, and
Jason is handling them quite nicely. From this perspective,
Jason is a very *good* speller.

Is Your Child Spelling on Grade Level?

Would you like to know whether Jason, or your child in
second through eighth grade is spelling on grade level? Researchers who look at thousands of samples of children's
writing are able to identify some general patterns and high-
frequency words that kids use in their writing at various

grade levels. While these are only general markers, you can compare your child's progress with what writers generally learn at a particular grade level. Expect there to be overlap from one grade level to the next. For example, whether or not to double the consonant before adding an ending might be worked on in both second and third grades. Likewise, third graders are more concerned with compound words like *bluebird* and *inside*, while fifth graders make decisions about spelling compounds like *twenty-one, post office*, and *applesauce*. There is no precise list of words or skills that must be addressed at a particular grade level, but there are general markers to indicate if kids are developmentally on track. The following indicates some important guideposts that you can look for when informally assessing your child's spelling development:

Second graders should be mastering these kinds of patterns:

Short vowel patterns in words like *sat, men, did, mom, cup,* and *cash.*

Long vowel patterns in words like *made, nail, gray, sleep, clean, hide, dime, bright, might, dry, hope, nose, boat, show,* and *cone.*

Consonant blends such as those made with *s, l,* and *r* in words like *stay, spot, black, glass, bring,* and *frog.*

Plurals formed by -*s* and -*es* in words like *lips, eyes, birds, horses,* and *classes.*

The endings -*ed* and -*ing* in words like *wanted, played, rained, eating, making, doing, riding,* and *running.*

Compound words such as *inside, baseball, rain-coat,* and *bluebird.*

Third graders should be mastering these kinds of patterns:

Plurals formed by -*s* and -*es* in words like *legs, bushes, cages,* and *porches.*

Consonant blends such as *scr, tch, str,* and *thr* in words like *scratch, scream, stretch,* and *thread.*

Short vowels in words like *camp, clock, shock, kept,* and *west.*

Long vowels in words like *paint, pony, own, bright, grew,* and *rule.*

Combinations such as -*au-,* -*al-,* and -*oi-,* in words like *taught, walking,* and *oil.*

R-controlled vowels in words like *hair, pear, cheer,* and *fare.*

Contractions and compound words in words like *didn't, weren't, football,* and *grandmother.*

Special spellings of sounds like the *s* and *j* sounds in words like *circle, pass, giant,* and *join.*

Prefixes in words like *unhappy, preheat, unable,* and *repaint.*

Fourth graders should be mastering these kinds of patterns:

Contractions such as *o'clock, you're, doesn't,* and *haven't.*

Long vowels in words like *trapeze, antelope, tune, drew,* and *explode.*

Compound words such as *good-bye, fireplace, T-shirt,* and *everybody.*

Special combinations such as the *squ, qu, dge, en,* and in words like *squeal, equal, bridge, chicken,* and *pumpkin.*

Possessives and plural possessives such as *mother's, animals'.*

Word endings such as *-ir, -ur, -al, -il,* and *-le.*

Suffixes such as *-ful, -less, -ment, -il,* and *-ness.*

Homographs (the same spelling for two different words, like "*record* player" and "*record* the date") such as *record, present,* and *content.*

Homophones such as *steel* and *steal; bored* and *board.*

Changing *y* to *i* in words like *prettiest, happiness, fries,* and *studies.*

Fifth graders should be mastering these kinds of patterns:

Possessives and plurals in words like *women's,* and changing *y* to *i* in words like *daisies.*

Unexpected spellings such as *modern, bargain, fashion,* and *habit.*

Silent *e, ei,* and *ie* in words like *clothe, receive, neighbor,* and *weight.*

Compound words such as *twenty-one, applesauce,* and *post office.*

Commonly misspelled words such as *sentence, chocolate, surely,* and *through.*

Lots of words with prefixes like *bi-, tri-, mid-, il-, im-, in-,* and *ir-.*

Lots of words with suffixes like *-er, -or, -ist, -ant, -am, -ist, -al,* and *-ous.*

Words with parts like *per-, pre-, pro-, -tion,* and *-cian.*

Words from other languages, like *ballet, cassette, stomach,* and *beret.*

Easily confused words like *recipe, seize, angle,* and *angel.*

Sixth graders should be mastering these kinds of patterns:

The more complex prefixes and suffixes, like *super-, over-, ad-, ac-, em-, en-, -ity, -ery, -ance,* and *-ence.*

Many word roots like *port* and *tract* in words like *transportation, import, opportunity, reporter, tractor, contraction,* and *distract.*

Words from other languages like *brochure, genre, mustache,* and *mosquito.*

Commonly misspelled words such as *license, choir, athlete,* and *grammar.*

Seventh graders should be mastering these kinds of patterns:

Unusual plurals such as *torpedoes, stereos,* and *fathers-in-law.*

Many word roots, such as *graph* in *cartography* and *seismograph; flu* in *fluency, fluctuate,* and *influential.*

Words from French like *physique, gourmet, plateau,* and *debut.*

Prefixes and suffixes such as *dec-, epi-, -able,* and *-ible.*

Related words such as *manager* and *managerial.*

Commonly misspelled words such as *conscience, stationery, occurring, gauge, vacuum,* and *advantageous.*

Words from Spanish such as *tortilla, lariat,* and *iguana.*

Greek roots such as *rhythmic, rhetoric, architect.*

Suffixes like *-cial* and *-tial* in words like *racial* and *martial.*

Words from other languages, such as *kindergarten, spaghetti, caboose,* and *ebony.*

Eighth graders should be mastering these kinds of patterns:

Words from names, such as *boycott, cologne, bologna,* and *tantalizing.*

Unusual plurals, such as *alumni, appendixes,* and *memorandums.*

Roots in words such as *dissent, sentinel,* and *dissension.*

Words from French, such as *souvenir, rendezvous, millionaire,* and *premiere.*

Prefixes and suffixes such as *dia-, -ics,* and *-ism.*

Easily confused words such as *allusion* and *illusion; immigration* and *emigration.*

Patterns based on meaning such as *expire* and *expiration; repeat* and *repetition;* and *reveal* and *revelation.*

Spellings from Greek sounds, as in *chloro-phyll, orphanage,* and *pseudonym.*

Middle Eastern and Asian words such as *bazaar, ketchup,* and *cheetah.*

Commonly misspelled words such as *congratulations, secede,* and *gaiety.*

Words from other languages, such as *gnu, guerrilla,* and *yacht.*

Ask your child and your child's teacher about the kind of word study he or she is involved in for spelling. Does the program somewhat match what you see outlined in this chapter? If not, find out what *is* being done to teach your child the patterns and consistency of English spelling. This is a part of your child's education that should not be neglected.

4

Is Your Child
on Grade Level?

Finding Your Child's
Spelling Level

Finding out your child's spelling level is like asking
"How tall are you?," "What time is it?," "What's the
temperature?," or "How much did it rain?" Sometimes
it's useful to measure these things.

Measuring spelling achievement is easy. To determine
your child's spelling level, administer the spelling test provided in this chapter.

A grade level in spelling is a unit of measure much
like inches, hours, or degrees of temperature. Spelling grade
level is determined by looking at what words children generally spell correctly in their writing at a given grade level
in school. Researchers interested in fourth grade level spelling, for example, might look at thousands of samples of
fourth grade writing and ask, "What words were misspelled
by these kids at the beginning of fourth grade that were
mastered by the end of fourth grade?" The words generated by this process would make up a fourth grade level
word list.

If I showed you thousands of samples of children's writing, I could demonstrate that *me* is a first grade word, *unknown* is a fifth grade word, and *financial* is an eighth grade word. This simply means that first graders learn to spell words similar in difficulty to *me*, fifth graders learn to spell words similar in difficulty to *unknown*, and eighth graders learn to spell words similar in difficulty to *financial*. Grouping words according to similarities in spelling difficulty allows us to measure a child's level of spelling development. Although this is a gross rather than an exact measure, the test is a strong indicator of performance.

Word list researchers look at other things too—like how many times kids use a particular word in their writing. *'Twas* isn't a very good word for a word list because kids never use it when they write. They rarely even see *'twas*, unless they happen to read "'Twas the Night Before Christmas."

The word lists in this chapter will help you get a general idea of your child's grade level of spelling proficiency. Keep in mind that this is an indicator, not an exact measure. Looking closely at your child's writing and monitoring how well he or she responds to spelling instruction at the level indicated will verify the grade equivalency placement indicated by this test.

Administering the Test

1. Introduce the test. "You are going to write some words to help us find out how well you can spell. Some of the words are hard to spell. Do your best. But do not worry if you don't know some of the words."

2. Offer help distinguishing between words. "Ask for a sentence only when you need one to know what word I'm calling. If I say 'red,' you might need a sentence to show if I mean 'a "red" dress' or if I mean 'She "read" a book.'

The Gentry Spelling Grade Level Placement Test

GRADE ONE

1. all	8. on	15. you
2. me	9. the	16. see
3. do	10. and	17. is
4. come	11. one	18. ten
5. play	12. be	19. was
6. at	13. like	20. no
7. yes	14. am	

GRADE TWO

1. jump	8. fine	15. hope
2. apple	9. off	16. much
3. five	10. bell	17. seven
4. other	11. say	18. egg
5. that	12. part	19. sometime
6. more	13. like	20. wall
7. house	14. brown	

GRADE THREE

1. spring	8. placed	15. airplane
2. helps	9. below	16. learn
3. farmer	10. walked	17. those
4. people	11. also	18. cream
5. bones	12. often	19. eight
6. saved	13. wrong	20. carry
7. roof	14. things	

GRADE FOUR

1. worry	8. blame	15. wrote
2. twenty	9. wreck	16. iron
3. you're	10. November	17. fifth
4. dozen	11. loud	18. tomorrow
5. thumb	12. wasn't	19. writing
6. carried	13. finish	20. frozen
7. surprise	14. middle	

The Gentry Spelling Grade Level Placement Test

GRADE FIVE

1. neighbor	8. hungry	15. library
2. parties	9. subject	16. yawn
3. rotten	10. claim	17. midnight
4. worst	11. unknown	18. steady
5. laid	12. American	19. prepare
6. manners	13. officer	20. village
7. parents	14. prove	

GRADE SIX

1. jewel	8. depot	15. hymn
2. thief	9. ruin	16. lettuce
3. avenue	10. yield	17. burden
4. arrangement	11. seize	18. canvas
5. theme	12. difference	19. grocery
6. system	13. interview	20. lawyer
7. written	14. zero	

GRADE SEVEN

1. possession	8. agriculture	15. straighten
2. yacht	9. scientist	16. establish
3. thorough	10. anchor	17. laboratory
4. gymnasium	11. announce	18. cashier
5. interrupt	12. revenue	19. wrath
6. athletic	13. patient	20. intelligent
7. secretary	14. pressure	

GRADE EIGHT

1. fierce	8. appropriateness	15. restaurant
2. analyze	9. cheetah	16. alliteration
3. committee	10. schedule	17. grievance
4. predominant	11. autobiographical	18. vengeance
5. pursue	12. executive	19. guarantee
6. chemically	13. coincidence	20. columnist
7. financial	14. seniority	

Remember, ask for a sentence only when you need one to help you know which word to write."

3. Have your child number a column one through twenty. "Begin by numbering your paper one through twenty."

4. Start where you think your child can correctly spell all the words in the list. This is usually one or two grade levels below your child's grade level placement if he or she functions on grade level.

5. Call out the word list. Watch as your child writes down each word you call out.

6. Stop when your child misses more than half the words in a list. (Only three or four consecutive lists are usually needed to find a child's placement.)

Scoring the Test
Find the list where your child spells at least ten words correctly. The highest grade level at which your child spells about 50 percent of the words is his or her approximate grade level for spelling placement.

An Example of How the Test is Scored
Kellyn is a second grader whose parents had questions about her spelling level when she brought home a first grade level spelling list on the first day of second grade. Her father administered the Gentry Spelling Grade Level Placement Test.

Look at Kellyn's test results. Her grade level scores are as follows:

SECOND GRADE: 100%   THIRD GRADE: 70%   FOURTH GRADE: 55%

1. Say	1. ✗ sring *spring*	1 ✗ woried *worried*
2 apples	2 helps	2 twenty
3 five	3 farmer	3 you're
4 other	4 ✗ poepla *people*	4 dozen
5 that	5 bones	5 ✗ tumb *thumb*
6. more	6 saved	6 ✗ carryed *carried*
7. house	7 ✗ rouff rufe ruph rouph *roof*	7 surprise
8 fine	8 place	8 blame
9 off	9 below	9 ✗ reck *wreck*
10. bell	10 ✗ walket *walked*	10 November
11. part	11 ✗ allsow *also*	11 loud
12 eight	12 often	12 ✗ wasent *wasn't*
13. brown	13 ✗ rong *wrong*	13 finish
14 hope	14 things	14 ✗ midle *middle*
15 much	15 airplane	15 wrote
16 seven	16 learn	16 iron
17. egg	17 those	17 ✗ fith *fifth*
18. Sometime	18 cream	18 ✗ tomorow *tomorrow*
19. wall	19 eight	19 writing
20. father	20 carry	20 frozun *frozen*

This test places Kellyn as a fourth grade level speller. The test reveals she knows much more about spelling than most second graders. Certainly, the first grade spelling list her teacher sent home would be much too easy for her. Kellyn's parents might share this information with her teacher to make sure Kellyn gets spelling instruction on an appropriate level.

We can verify the test results by analyzing Kellyn's spelling. A close look shows that Kellyn is indeed a very sophisticated speller, considering she is only in second grade. She spelled fourteen of the third grade words and eleven of the fourth grade words correctly. Look at her treatment of *roof:*

rouff–rufe–ruph–rouph

Kellyn knows sophisticated alternative spellings: the *ou* vowel digraph; the *e*-marker pattern; the use of *ff* at the end of a word; the use of *ph* for the /f/ sound. All of these are logical alternative spellings and she tries them in the appropriate context.

It's a good bet that Kellyn would benefit from instruction with some third and, mostly, fourth grade level words and word patterns.

How Important Are Spelling Grade Level Results?

Here's a reminder: Expert spelling ability is probably a genetic accident. Outside the context of providing developmentally appropriate instruction, *spelling grade level is not so important!* The goal for your child should be spelling consciousness—a habit of caring about expert spelling when spelling is important. Many children, no matter how hard they work, may never really achieve the status of expert speller. But that lack of achievement doesn't matter if they have spelling consciousness. Intrinsic desire for and concern about spelling (when correct spelling is important) will certainly at times be inconvenient for the naturally poor speller. But spelling consciousness—not expert spelling—is more closely tied to success. George Washington, Albert Einstein, Thomas Edison, Martin Luther King, Jr., and Queen Elizabeth I probably would have failed the grade level test. They were all lousy spellers who probably spelled below grade level!

5

Can Your Child Visualize Words?

Why Some Children Have Extreme Difficulty with Spelling, the "Spelling Gene," and the Golden Rule for Perfect Spelling

The ability to visualize words is the hallmark of an expert speller. Does your child have it? If not, he or she may have extreme difficulty with spelling. We know that the power of visualization is far stronger in some people than in others. Expert spellers use it—they see words in the mind's eye.

Imagine a drug that would signal the brain to store and retrieve visual images of words. Is such as drug far into the future? Is a "spelling gene" that alters some chemical process in the brain and triggers more efficient visualization of words, science fiction? Whether the spelling gene turns out to be reality or myth, it is a fact that expert spelling is, in part, a genetic accident!

Have you ever stood in an assembly singing next to someone who simply couldn't carry a tune? I think expert spelling works the same way. Both of these abilities, singing and spelling, may to some extent be genetically encoded. Singing comes naturally for some, while others can't do it very well. Likewise, storing and retrieving the exact visual forms of words is far more natural for some spellers than for others. Regardless of intelligence, level of training, or how someone is taught, the ability to sing in melodious refrain or to spell thousands of words with exactness is a "gift"—some people have it and some people don't. You might say that singers and expert spellers are born—not made!

While research may not be able to explain what enables expert spellers to spell with exactness, it's easy to see what the poor speller can not do. Lousy spellers can't see words in their mind's eye. The brain's ability to form mental pictures of words and to retrieve them is lacking. This ability has been called the "visual coding mechanism." Children display a wide range of ability for it, and it probably can't be taught.

Forming Visual Images of Words

Try this experiment. Read each phrase below and fill in the blank with a word that sounds exactly like the name of a vegetable. (Hint: The vegetable is the orange edible root preferred by rabbits.) Now close your eyes and try to visualize the correct spelling of the word that goes in the blank. (Most expert spellers visualize words in typed print, not in handwritten cursive, so try to "see" the word in typed print.)

1. A ring of twenty-four _____ gold.
2. A two _____ diamond.
3. The rabbit ate the _____.
4. The mark ∧ , used to show where an addition is to be made in text, is a _____.

If you could spell three or four of the words, you probably used your visual coding mechanism to see the word in you mind's eye. You may not have known that "caret" is the name for ∧. In that case, your visual coding mechanism may not be at fault, you are just uninstructed in "carets."

Expert spellers can spell *karat, carat, carrot,* and *caret* by "seeing" them. If you are a lousy speller, you may have been unable to "see" any of these words—poor spellers have a tough time seeing words in their mind's eye. Perhaps you resorted to the poor speller's strategy: you spelled it like it sounds. Poor spellers don't do well on the "carrot" test because *karat, carat, carrot,* and *caret,* all sound exactly alike! Your brain must recall the visual form to spell these words correctly.

Is Your Child a Visually Challenged Speller?

It's very easy to determine if your child has difficulty forming visual images of words. Just look at his or her spelling. A child who is having difficulty will produce spelling that does not match what occurs normally and he or she will not use a consistent strategy.

In order to check your child's visual coding ability, let's look at spellings by a fourth grader who appears to have processing difficulty with spelling. Studying his case will help you understand what to look for in your child. Note that this child is intelligent and reads on grade level. Nevertheless, he doesn't seem to be able to visualize words. Look at his spellings:

JOD	for	*job*
GROPE	for	*group's*
FIRS	for	*first*
TOMP	for	*top*
CHAR	for	*chart*
LAT BAGS	for	*ladybugs*

Now look at his spellings as they appeared in context:

He reads these instructions: *What job was your group asked to do?*

He writes: My JOD was to help get ARE GROPE ANSER.

He reads these instructions: *Now look at the ladybugs on page 2. Estimate how many ladybugs are shown. Write how you would explain to a friend how you found your estimate of the number of ladybugs.*

He writes: What I did FRIS is I CONTED THE SQARS on the chart. I CONTED to four SQUARS on the SIAD then I CONTED the SQUARS on TOMP. Then I TIMEED 4 x 4. That would = 16. Then I put the CHAR on the LAT BAGS. Then I PICK a SQAR. You would CONT the LAT BAGS in the SQUAR. I got 23 in my SQAR. So then I times 23 and 16. So 23 x 16 = 368. So that is how I would get A ASER like that.

Even if we analyze all twenty-five misspellings, we can see that this child's spelling does not match normally occurring developmental strategies or stages:

His spelling is much more sophisticated than a Stage 1 speller's would be.

He is not a Stage 2 speller. (Stage 2 spellers spell by ear, but they produce abbreviated spellings because they leave out sounds.) This speller is a more experienced and more sophisticated speller than most Stage 2 spellers. And, while Stage 2 spellers *consistently* provide a partial mapping of letters to sounds, this speller's strategies vary. Even though he sometimes leaves out sounds—FRIS for *first,* CHAR for *chart,* PICK for *picked,* and ASER for *answer*— it's sporadic and unpredictable rather than a consistent strategy. Notice the lapses in this speller's power to represent sounds in words: He spells *answer* as A-N-S-E-R the first time but ASER the next. He spells *chart* correctly the first time, but then spells it CHAR. He doesn't even notice the difference.

He is not a Stage 3 speller. (Stage 3 spellers spell by ear.) Although he does occasionally spell by ear—LAT for *lady*, SQUAR for *square*—this is not a consistent strategy.

He is not a Stage 4 speller. (Stage 4 spellers spell by eye.) Although he does spell by eye sporadically (GROPE is a familiar visual pattern, albeit the wrong pattern for *group's*; SIAD for *said* and TIMEED for *times* are visual spellings), he doesn't spell by eye consistently enough to call it a dominant strategy. In fact, what is woefully apparent is that this boy usually has problems spelling by eye—his mind's eye doesn't recognize when his spellings are way off base.

An Oblivious Hodgepodge and a Lack of Visualization

I would describe this challenged speller as one whose ability to see words in his mind is weak and faulty. He uses a hodgepodge of strategies, but seems oblivious to which strategies work best. What really marks him as a severely challenged speller is that he is much weaker at visualizing or forming mental pictures of words than other spellers of his age, ability level, and training.

Look at these examples: He read *job* in the instructions, then immediately wrote JOD. He read *ladybugs* three times in the instructions, but almost immediately lost any visual memory he might have formed of the word. He spelled it as two words—LAT BAGS. For someone who can read at fourth grade level, LAT BAGS isn't even close—and this speller used it twice!

Another interesting example of this child's empty storehouse of visual images of words is his misuse of spelling patterns that most kids his age and ability level use automatically. He seems oblivious to his own misuse of easy patterns, such as -*op* (as in *top*, *hop*, and *stop*), -*ug* (as in *bug*, *rug*, and *hug*), -*ag* (as in *bag*, *tag*, and *rag*), -*ope* (as in *hope*, *rope*, and *dope*.) He doesn't "see" that these patterns are misused.

Is Your Child a Genius?

If your child's spelling looks like this child's, please don't lose hope. It's no discredit not to have visual word memory. Your son or daughter may be brilliant! Einstein, Edison, Washington, Queen Elizabeth I, and Martin Luther King, Jr. to some extent all shared this trait. Simply put, if your son or daughter doesn't have the "spelling gene," it's just an inconvenience.

The Rule for Perfect Spelling

Here's the golden rule for perfect spelling:

All words must be spelled as they look!

If your son or daughter can't form mental pictures of words, here's how you can help:

1. Make spelling consciousness a habit.
Anyone can be a good speller if they have spelling consciousness—a habit of care for expert spelling and a desire for and concern about it. Spelling consciousness *works*—but it is an inconvenience.

Lots of everyday activities are an inconvenience. Spelling consciousness needs to be a habit in your houschold, like brushing teeth, taking a bath, eating, exercising, getting a haircut, clipping toenails, ad infinitum. As a parent, you help your kids learn to do these things from habit. Poor spellers simply add one more habit to the list: They practice spelling consciousness.

It's hard to make taking a bath a habit if the water is freezing cold. The habit of getting a haircut is easier once kids figure out it doesn't hurt. Kids like painless habits, so help your son or daughter make spelling consciousness a habit by taking the pain out of it.

2. Make sure your son or daughter gets help.

If you need a phone number and can't remember it, what do you do? You get help. You might *ask someone*. You might *look it up* in the phone book. You might *use technology* by pressing a couple of buttons to get a listing recorded on your call identifier, in your telephone memory, or in your personal computer. If all else fails, you can always call the directory assistance operator for *professional help*. Asking someone, looking it up, using technology, and getting professional help are also easy ways to get help with spelling.

Four Easy Ways to Get Help with Spelling

1. Ask someone who can spell. You may think this is a bad habit, but it is really one of the best recommendations I can make. An extremely poor speller should not be reluctant to ask for help. By about fourth grade, kids are expected to be able to produce a piece of writing with near-perfect spelling. Make sure that your child with severe spelling difficulty is not ashamed to ask for help. It's *smart* to ask for help!

Asking for help is a real-life strategy. An acquaintance told me about sending out her wedding invitations. She wrote them by hand to impress her guests. Unfortunately, she wasn't a good speller and she didn't ask for help. Imagine her embarrassment when she discovered the in-laws' first impression—the misspelling of *rehearsal* in her handwritten note. Too bad she didn't ask someone for help: "Could you read over this before I send it?" Asking for help is just plain smart!

2. Look it up in the dictionary. Often a poor speller *does* know enough about the word to find it in the dictionary. People complain that poor spellers can't find words in the dictionary, but more times than not, they *can* find the unknown word. Looking up words in the dictionary is a good strategy if there are only a few words to look up.

3. Use technology. Technology is making it easier for poor spellers to practice spelling consciousness. The computer spelling checker is a great boon for the poor speller. The sooner your son or daughter learns to write on a computer, the better.

Many kids love using the hand-held Franklin speller® when writing. These "calculators" for spelling even come with voice technology—a child types in a word and the speller spells and pronounces a list of alternatives. The child picks the word that fits. Franklin spellers® are relatively inexpensive and great devices for poor spellers.

4. Get Professional help. Your son or daughter may need "professional" help. I'm recommending an editor, not a psychiatrist! Most professional writers couldn't get along without a good editor. Poor spellers *need* editing help. Consider offering to be your child's editor. You can help by cheerfully editing for spelling whenever your child asks for help.

Once you have helped your son or daughter learn about spelling consciousness and have shown him or her easy ways to get help, don't be afraid to find out what kind of instruction your child is getting in school. The key is to individualize instruction for the severely challenged speller and to make instruction developmentally appropriate. Consider the widely practiced policy of studying from word lists. The fourth grader in the case study reviewed in this chapter needs his own personal word list. Fourth grade spelling lists generally look like this:

trapeze	prettiest	steal	squeal
antelope	fries	steel	bridge
explode	happiness	bored	chicken

Even though this struggling speller can read on grade level, he is not recognizing his own misspellings of first grade level spelling patterns. The pattern-to-pattern word study and word learning list most appropriate for him might look more like this:

sat	made	played	glass
cup	gray	rained	black
cash	sheep	running	frog

Studying words with these patterns will be much more beneficial for this boy at this point in his development than using the grade-appropriate fourth grade word list, which would only frustrate and confuse him.

Help your child survive as a severely challenged speller. Teach your child spelling consciousness. Teach him or her the golden rule for perfect spelling: All words must be spelled as they look! Finally, teach the four actions that make it easy to spell with absolute perfection:

- Ask a good speller
- Look it up
- Use technology
- Get professional help

6

How to Identify a
Really Bad Spelling Lesson

A Gentle Reminder to Your Child's Teacher: Please Pay Attention to Spelling

Is your child struggling with spelling lessons that do more harm than good? Is he or she being *assigned* spelling but not really being *taught?* Assignments that are boring and time-consuming turn spelling study into drudgery. You will recognize these assignments as busywork. Instead of helping kids master spelling and develop spelling consciousness, such lessons make kids hate spelling.

I think it's helpful for parents to recognize really bad spelling lessons so they can help the teacher avoid them. Sometimes bringing your child's spelling to the teacher's attention helps the teacher choose more appropriate spelling instruction. Here's what you need to look for if you suspect that your child's spelling lessons don't work:

Telltale Signs of a Really Bad Spelling Lesson

1. The word list is either much too hard or much too easy for your child.

2. Lesson content is inappropriate: your child is not learning the spelling concepts or words and patterns that he or she is likely to use when writing.

3. The activities are busywork and your child complains a lot about doing them.

4. Your child is spending a lot of time working on spelling, but isn't learning how to be a better speller.

5. The teacher isn't paying much attention to what your child is doing.

An example of a really bad spelling lesson:

Blake is in fourth grade. Here's his spelling lesson for one week, which consisted of a twenty-word word list and a "spelling relay" work sheet. (The grade designations list will be explained below.)

Blake's Spelling List

1. cardinal	(Grade 5)	11. flowering	(Grade 4)
2. ordinal	(not listed)	12. fibrous root	(not listed)
3. directions	(Grade 6)	13. character	(Grade 7)
4. globe	(Grade 4)	14. geography	(Grade 6)
5. North America	(Grade 4)	15. place value	(Grade 6)
6. telescope	(Grade 7)	16. million	(Grade 5)
7. construct	(Grade 6)	17. organizer	(Grade 8)
8. equipment	(Grade 5)	18. glossary	(Grade 7)
9. sequence	(Grade 7)	19. dictionary	(Grade 6)
10. conifer	(not listed)	20. vocabulary	(Grade 7)

During the week, Blake's work sheet instructed him to copy the words, rewrite them in alphabetical order, divide them into syllables, use each in a sentence, and take a spelling test. Let's see how his assignment holds up against the telltale signs of a really bad spelling lesson:

1. Question: *Does the word list match Blake's spelling level?*

Answer: No.

Blake spells on about fourth grade level. The list of words is much too hard for him. Note the grade level shown in parentheses after each word. This is the grade level most often reported as being the appropriate level at which that word might be taught.

After checking twelve spelling series and other word list sources, I found only three of the assigned words to be appropriate for fourth grade spelling: *globe, North America,* and perhaps *flowering.* (Actually, *flower* would be fourth grade level, but *flowering* isn't often used by fourth grade writers.) Fourteen of the words would typically be taught in fifth to eighth grade. *Ordinal, conifer,* and *fibrous root* are not even listed in the twelve spelling sources I surveyed.

You don't need spelling word lists to determine if your child's assigned words are appropriate. Ask yourself this question: Do the words in my child's spelling assignment match the kind of words he or she misspells when writing? Here's an example of how I used this question to check Blake's spelling list.

I found five misspelled words in the twenty sentences Blake wrote for the previous week's spelling assignment:

PERTTY	for	*pretty*
WHOULD	for	*would*
DOE'S	for	*does*
TRACKTOR	for	*tractor*
STORES	for	*stories*

① North Carolina is a Blake
very pretty state to
live in.

⑤ If I had an invention
I would make a
thing that does work.

⑥ I know how to drive
a tracktor.

⑦ I love to write stores
about Dinosaurs

These are, in fact, mostly third and fourth grade words. They are words Blake will use often in his writing. (Even though *tractor* is not a high-frequency word, it's a good spelling word for Blake because he likes to write about tractors.) Does the difficulty level of words Blake misspells in his writing match the difficulty level of words on the spelling list?

Spelling words from writing	Assigned spelling list
pretty	ordinal
would	conifer
stories	fibrous root

The answer is "no"! *Ordinal, conifer,* and *fibrous root* are not good study words for a child who misspells *would, pretty,* and *stories.* Although Blake might memorize the assigned words and make 100 percent on the spelling test, the assigned list will have a limited impact on helping him develop as a speller. The assignment reduces spelling to rote memorization. It provides little opportunity for learning the patterns and consistency of English spelling.

2. Question: *Does the assigned word list reflect good spelling content—something worth knowing about spelling?*

Answer: Not really.

The words Blake misspelled in his writing—*pretty, would, does,* and *stories*—do lend themselves to lessons in which something worth knowing about spelling could be taught:

WORD	CONTENT
pretty	Fourth graders might benefit from studying words that start with *pre-* versus *per-*. (Blake probably misspelled *pretty* because he pronounces it "per-tee.")
would	Fourth graders might benefit from studying *w* words like *would, weather, Wednesday, what's, wheel, where,* and *whenever.* (*W* words are particularly troublesome for young spellers.)
does	Fourth graders might benefit from studying words with unusual spellings like *does* (*v.*, third person singular present indicative of *do*) and *does* (*n.*, plural of *doe*). (Blake's spelling DOE'S shows he is confused about contractions.)
stories	Fourth graders might benefit from studying when to "change the *y* to *i* and add *es* to form plurals.

While the assigned list relates to various subject areas of study, such as math, science, geography, and English, these words might best be taught as new vocabulary. They provide little opportunity for Blake to develop concepts about spelling.

3. Question: *Did Blake complain about doing the assignment?*

Answer: Yes.

Blake did complain. He recognized that the assignment was busywork. When he won a "homework pass" the following week in school, he used it to get out of doing *spelling* homework. Most of the activities suggested on the work sheet have limited value in helping Blake learn to spell the assigned words.

- Simply listing words is busywork. It's not a good way to learn to spell.

- Rewriting words in alphabetical order is busywork. It helps very little with learning to spell.

- Dividing words into syllables isn't the most efficient way to learn to spell words. The time required to locate all twenty words in the dictionary would be better spent in a "Look–say–cover and visualize–write–check" technique (see Appendix B). Dividing words into syllables does help with spelling some words. The teacher might provide syllable divisions on the original assignment sheet, which would allow the kids to spend their time using strategies to *study* the words, rather than wasting a lot of time looking them up. Although kids should practice looking up words occasionally to develop dictionary skills, looking up twenty words every week is boring.

- Writing sentences for spelling words every week is boring. Spelling words should be words kids *already* use in their writing, but can't yet spell correctly. Writing sentences doesn't help much to learn to spell the words.

4. Question: *Is Blake becoming a better speller?*

Answer: Things could be better!

Blake is developing some sloppy habits as a speller: He's rushing through his homework and misspelling the assigned words in the busywork activities. Even though he commits *conifer, fibrous root,* and *ordinal* to short-term memory for the test, he will not use these words when he writes and will probably forget how to spell them. The "conifer–fibrous root" lesson does not allow him to learn important spelling content needed by fourth grade spellers.

5. Question: *Is Blake's teacher paying attention to his spelling?*

Answer: She needs to pay closer attention to spelling.

It is not necessary for teachers to grade every piece of work students produce. Some work is for practice. Think of the practice needed for becoming a star football player or a great concert pianist; there is an appropriate time for both practice and performance. While evaluation takes precedence during performance, great coaches and piano teachers do pay attention to their students in practice. Paying attention to the individual student's spelling is an appropriate role for the teacher. A quick spot-check of Blake's spelling assignment would have revealed some problems he was having.

Blake's teacher did look at his assigned spelling work. She marked it "O.K." in red ink. But she didn't pay much attention to what he was doing. She didn't find misspelled assigned words on Monday when he copied the word list for the week. She didn't find misspelled assigned words on Tuesday when he put them in alphabetical order. She apparently didn't notice PERTY, DOE'S, and WHOULD when she looked over his spelling sentences, or it didn't occur to her that these words did not match Blake's spelling assignments. One might conclude that Blake's teacher relegated spelling to the realm of busywork without paying much attention to it. Her strategy was to assign and test words without giving much attention to *teaching* them.

If you find a similar set of circumstances occurring with your child, I recommend that you find a gentle and nonthreatening way to discuss it with the teacher. Just bringing your child's spelling to the teacher's attention might be the first step in solving the problem.

Teachers face monumental expectations. Spelling, which has traditionally been assigned and not taught, is a subject many teachers need to be gently reminded to teach. Some teachers need to be reminded to pay attention to spelling. If you find your child trapped in a situation similar to Blake's, share this chapter with your child's teacher and ask what *you* can do to help your child with spelling.

7

Spelling and Academic Disaster

Scott's Story

Eileen Peterson understands the frustrating life of the struggling speller. She told me the story of her personal quest to help her son cope with his spelling disability. In spite of an endless stream of teacher conferences, countless hours commuting to tutoring sessions, high tutoring costs, and contradictory advice from teachers and experts; in spite of watching her son struggle while his self-esteem plummeted; in spite of doing everything in her power, but finding no solutions for her son's spelling problems—Mrs. Peterson managed to find some humor in the situation:

> Oh, we tried out technology. I heard about those hand-held spelling "calculators" designed to check words for spelling. "Just what Scott, needs," I thought. "I'll pay anything for it."
>
> We went down and purchased the Franklin *Spelling Ace® Plus*. Scott was so enthusiastic, he opened the box when he got back to the car.

On the drive home from purchasing the spell checker, Scott said, "Mom, call out some words I misspelled in my writing." Picture it, I'm driving, he's punching in spelling, and his sister is sitting there watching.

I first call out "come" and he punches in C–O–M–B. The *Spelling Ace® Plus* light flashes up: "Correct!"

My next word is "hurt" and he punches in H–E–A–R–T. The *Spelling Ace® Plus* light flashes up: "Correct!"

Next, "roam." R–O–M–E. "Correct!"

His sister is giggling, but I am not laughing.

My next word is "does." Scott tries punching it in twice:

D–O–S–E. "Correct!" D–O–U–S–E. "Correct!"

By this time his sister thinks the scene is hilarious. "Take." T–A–C–K. "Correct!"

"Various." V–A–R–I–E–S. "Correct!"

I thought, "I can't believe this!" I wrote Scott's responses on the "User's Guide" cover. I was so amazed. I can show it to you. I saved it!

There is much that is not so amusing about Scott's history with spelling and its impact on his schooling. His mother was more than willing to share Scott's story:

Kindergarten—It's "Coming Later"

Scott seemed to struggle from the beginning. Even though his parents knew he was bright, he only made two "Outstanding's" (for knowing colors and shapes) out of the sixty-four ratings on his kindergarten report card. The rest of his ratings were S's ("Satisfactory"). There was one exception. In the second term, his "interest in using letters to make words" (i.e., spelling) was rated C, which, according to the report key, means "Coming later." At the end of kindergarten, his father and mother questioned whether Scott should repeat kindergarten. His teacher recommended he be promoted to first grade.

First Grade—A Disaster

Early in the year Scott's first grade teacher gave mixed messages about his performance. He had a preference for drawing but struggled to write three-word sentences. His parents read to him nightly, but he didn't like to read to them because the material was frustrating. Scott had always been focused and attentive at home, but his teacher reported that he couldn't sit still during "circle time." His self-image soon hit the bottom. In March, he was placed in the "Chapter One" reading program for extra help in basic skills.

At that time, his teacher reported "retention would be in his best interest." She said that Scott would be "at risk for success and happiness in second grade." His parents requested extensive testing to help them decide whether Scott should be retained or promoted. The principal approved an evaluation. A copy of Scott's "Pupil Evaluation Team Referral" lists him as "developmentally young," "unable to attend," "overactive," and prone "to daydream a lot," but the IQ test confirmed that Scott was "bright."

Scott's Verbal and Numerical Memory skills on the McCarthy Scales of Children's Abilities were one and one-half years *above* his chronological age. The Kaufman Test of Educational Achievement indicated excellent math, average reading, but *extremely low* scores in *spelling*. During the math test, the tester noted that Scott made six number reversals: instead of "12" he would write "21."

First grade was a disaster. The teacher who said that Scott's reading and writing were fine in September had put him in Chapter One for special help seven months later. In order to "assist him in learning to decode sounds," the school-district level special services tester recommended changing Scott's reading instruction. The certified special education consultant recommended "appropriate instructional methodology" for reading, but never said what that was. The retention/promotion decision process had begun as early as March. After Scott endured hours of individual testing and classroom observation by outside evaluators, the teacher recommended retention; the psychologist recommended promotion.

Scott was still struggling. "I want to go to second grade but I want to read better," he told his mother. Ironically, on June 7, Scott's parents received a letter from the Chapter One reading program assistant: "We feel that Scott has improved in this area this year and will not need Chapter One reading services next year." Exhausted, dismayed, and frustrated, the Petersons signed Scott up for a summer tutoring program at a special "learning center." They commuted for one-half hour, three days a week throughout the summer and "spent a fortune" on tutoring. Scott received a dose of intensive phonics and memorized a list of primer and preprimer words. At the end of the summer he still spelled *went* as WANT.

Second Grade—From "Wow" to "Nothing to Worry About"

Scott was promoted to a combination first and second grade class. He wasn't connecting with reading and writing. His self-esteem was still in the pits. He repeatedly told his parents he was "stupid." His mother recalls, "He hated reading and writing."

There continued to be lots of opinions about Scott's academic problems—all full of inconsistencies:

"I think he has a learning disability."

"Nothing to worry about."

"Wow, what wonderful gains Scott has made this year."

"He's so bright, he'll learn to compensate as he learns naturally."

On the California Achievement Test, Scott scored at the 98th percentile in science but dipped to the 15th percentile in spelling. He couldn't spell simple words and his parents continued to worry.

Third Grade–A Great Teacher, A New Beginning

Scott entered a new school and ended up with what his mother described as an "incredible" language arts teacher, Marsha Winship. "He became a writer and a reader," his mother reported. "He also became a speaker—confident and competent." It shows what a positive impact one teacher can have on a child's life. Ms. Winship highlighted Scott's successes. "Scott is a 'treasure' in any classroom," she wrote on his report card. Ms. Winship didn't focus on spelling, but she did pay attention to it, and Scott learned to write in spite of his limitations as a speller. She lit a fire inside him that made reading and writing exciting.

Ms. Winship put Scott on a path to academic success. He has continued to be a reader and writer and to achieve academic success in every area—except spelling. Now in sixth grade, Scott is a cool guy. He's "really into sailing." He's an avid reader and writer. Even though he continues to be a lousy speller, his teachers consistently notice his talents.

Severe spelling disability, as described in Chapter 5, is recognizable given a combination of history and performance like Scott's. He's very bright and achieves in all areas—except spelling. He has a noticeable processing difficulty related exclusively to spelling and exhibits the patterns of severe spelling disability, as described below:

How I Know Scott Has a Spelling Disability

1. He cannot see words in his mind's eye.
2. His spellings do not match one of the normally occurring developmental stages (Stage 1 through Stage 4, as described in Chapters 2 and 5).

3. He uses a hodgepodge of unpredictable and sporadic strategies rather than consistent ones.
4. He cannot produce spellings appropriate for his age and ability level.
5. He seems to have lapses in his power to represent words.
6. He exhibits an empty storehouse of visual images of words.
7. He seems to be oblivious to which strategies (i.e., spelling by ear, spelling by eye, spelling by pattern, spelling by analogy to known words) work best.
8. When attempting to spell by eye, he frequently uses visual patterns that do not fit.
9. He uses fragmented spelling patterns.
10. He uses spellings that are way off base.

Of course, the disability affects other areas—learning to read, facility at writing, perceptions of teachers and adults, scores on tests, self-esteem—but Scott's basic problem can be pinpointed: He has difficulty storing and retrieving the visual form of words. He can see and read words like *that*, *went*, and *they* thousands of times, but when he attempts to spell them, his brain is not able to process in the way that normally functioning spellers process words. Let's look at a few of Scott's samples.

The informal spelling test administered to Scott is revealing. When Scott took the test, he was entering sixth grade as a bright youngster who functioned at or above grade level in all other areas.

Scott's Sixth Grade Spelling Scores

Grade Level	Percentage Correct
1	95 percent
2	85 percent
3	64 percent
4	**52 percent**
5	24 percent

Scott is spelling at about fourth grade level. A look at the Grade Five list shows a general breakdown in his ability to store and retrieve the visual form of these words.

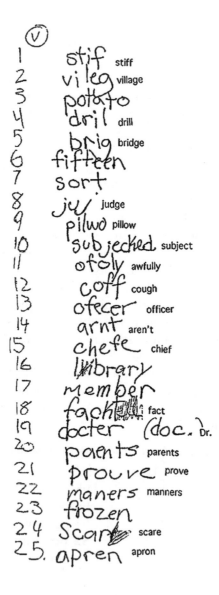

Notice these examples of really poor visual memory of words and inconsistent strategies:

PAENTS	for	*parents*	Stage Two
OFOLY	for	*awfully*	Stage Three
VILEG	for	*village*	Stage Three
PILWO	for	*pillow*	Stage Four
CHEFE	for	*chief*	Stage Four
PROUVE	for	*prove*	Stage Four
FACKT	for	*fact*	Stage Four

Even short samples of Scott's Fifth Grade writing reveal many of the characteristics listed under "How I Know Scott Has a Spelling Disability":

List the topic you knew a little about:
Scott writes: Larry Bird
Write your question about this:
Scott writes: What led him to be FAMOS?
Read and choose important information about this question. Write the answer in your own words:
Scott writes: Rebounds, step back MOV, 3 POUNS jump SOOTS, PASES, and last SEC 3 POUNTERS. HE just great ALAROUND basketball player.

If your son or daughter is a severely challenged speller, perhaps you have some of the same questions Mrs. Peterson asked me about Scott:

Question: *Does Scott have a learning disability?*

Answer: I would describe Scott's problem as a *spelling* disability. He experiences processing difficulties exclusive and specific to spelling.

Question: *Is there a genetic basis for Scott's spelling?*

Answer: I believe expert spellers are born, not made. Many of us will never be expert spellers no matter how hard we work at it. In that context, I would say there is a genetic basis for spelling ability. On the other hand, there is also a "nurture," or environmental, basis. All spellers can be better spellers if they work at it.

Scott will always have some difficulty with spelling.

Question: *How can Scott feel so smart and so dumb at the same time?*

Answer: Scott's history has lead to a lot of personal confusion about what has happened to him. He doesn't really understand why he has such difficulty with spelling. It isn't unusual for children who are gifted in some areas but struggling in others to feel insecure. In Scott's case, he needs reassurance that even though spelling will be an inconvenience, he can be successful. His teacher, Ms. Winship, was able to provide that type of reassurance, which in turn led to Scott's academic success.

Question: *During Scott's first and second grade experience, the statement "He will learn to compensate as he develops naturally" really upset us. We watched our son struggle and feel less capable than his peers. Why should a child have to figure it out by himself when someone who has the skills and knowledge could help him break the code for reading and writing and give him strategies to increase his success?*

Answer: I don't agree with the statement "He will learn to compensate as he develops naturally." As I stated in Chapter 1, teachers should help kids break the alphabet code. Teachers should follow Ms. Winship's example and give children strategies to increase success.

Question: *Why didn't anyone know the best approach to teach Scott? He has always tried so hard to be a phonetic reader/speller, even when he had no rules to work with. Sometimes he works so hard at decoding or spelling a word. We can see exactly how he comes up with the result—but it's incorrect.*

Answer: Reading and spelling are complex. They are much more complex than "rules" or "sounding out." There are lots of ways to teach reading, and children respond differently to various methods. How well a method works depends on lot of variables—whether it is meaningful; whether the child has the necessary knowledge, such as knowledge of the alphabet and phonemic awareness, to respond to the method; whether other factors are interfering; whether the child is excited by the process; whether he or she has good self-esteem and a feeling of success—to name a few. Ms. Winship was the first teacher Scott encountered who knew enough about individual differences and teaching reading to provide the skills, environment, and excitement needed for Scott's success. (No doubt, some of what had been done previously helped pave the way for his success.) I wish all teachers were like Ms. Winship.

For Scott, learning to read was much more difficult due to his inability to store and retrieve the visual form of words and spelling patterns. There probably weren't any easy solutions for Scott.

Question: *Scott has had a broad exposure to many topics and experiences. Why did test results indicate problems with "verbal associative thinking and general comprehension of facts," "circumlocutionary speech," "a significant weakness...in his fund of general information," and "a significant weakness in long-term language-based memory from experience in school"?*

Answer: The test results or the interpretation of the results were not valid. Scott doesn't have these problems. Some of the diagnostic impressions of the testers were erroneous.

Question: *When a child is very bright but has a spelling disability, is a "special education" label appropriate?*

Answer: Not in the general sense of "special education." Scott is not a slow learner. Scott did need special help from a reading teacher sensitive to his spelling disability.

Question: *Does Scott have a visual memory problem?*

Answer: Your diagnosis is closer to being accurate than the diagnosis of some of the experts. Scott has a problem storing and retrieving the visual form of words. As far as I can tell, his visual memory problem is specific to spelling.

Question: *We continue to be concerned that Scott works very hard, but spelling slows him down for reading and writing. What should be done?*

Answer: Follow the suggestions provided in Chapter 5. Spelling will always be an inconvenience for Scott, but if he develops spelling consciousness, he can do whatever he wants.

Will Scott Succeed?

I decided to end this chapter with two pieces of Scott's writing. With help—asking someone, using the dictionary, using technology, and relying on an editor—Scott will be able to correct his spelling.

Bosnia

On Sunday, NATO fired CRUIS missiles at SERBS radar, communication stations and ANTE-aircraft missile sites. Right after the missiles struck, the Bosnians took advantage of the Serbs weakness and went over and bombed their HEAAD city. The Serbs said when NATO fired missiles THE KILLD MENEY INOSENT people. The Serbs also said NATO was FITEING on the Bosnian side and THET they WOUL'D probably not TOLCK peace with NATO. The Serbs refused the NATO demands to remove WEPONS away from Sarajevo. The Serbs said that THAY would let the Bosnians and NATO have a better chance to kill them if they removed their guns.

* * * * * * * * *

"Fish, fresh fish!" YELED the fish SELER at the MARKAT place. It was a BETIFUL day in Miami, FLORDA. This BUTAFUL day was to be the day of the big 14 RAGATA. Tom Sole* was one of the best 14 SKIPERS in the state of Florida. His CROW was Jon Sumers, another well NONE SAILER. All the people were TALIKING about HAW Tom and Jon would win the race. The race started at 1:00. "Jon and I were SUPOSTED to be here at 12:00 to RIGE up. WHARE is he!" thought Tom to himself as he stood on the dock.

*(a racer in the RAGATA)

Scott's writing reflects what this bright eleven-year-old is thinking. What will happen to Scott? Maybe he will become president and solve world problems. Maybe he will be a great novelist.

Spelling will continue to be an inconvenience for Scott, but if he engages in developmentally appropriate word study, his spelling will improve. Scott's goal should be to develop good spelling habits. He should know when to make sure his writing is correctly spelled, and he should know how to get help to correct his spelling.

8

Supporting Your Child's Education

A Few Commonsense Guidelines for Parents

Although this book is about spelling, it is difficult to think about spelling without considering some of the broader issues related to parenting and schooling. Here are some general commonsense guidelines worth reviewing:

1. Turn off the television.

Remember second grader Blake's admonition about watching television? "Don't watch TV. It is bad for your brain."

As it turns out, Blake was right. Research suggests that television impedes the brain's development. Think about this statistic: by age five, the average child in the United States has watched 6,000 hours of television.

Evolution's End, Joseph Chilton Pearce's synthesis of twenty years of research into human intelligence, reports that Americans "spend more time looking at television than attending school." Pearce is convinced that this sobering fact has adverse effects on the development of human intelligence. It's not even the programming content that troubles Pearce most. Although he is concerned that your teenager will have seen 8,000 murders on television, and that studies show a direct correspondence between violence on television and violent behavior, the real problem is how television damages neurological development. Instead of a developing brain that is highly imaginative and full of imagery, television, according to Pearce, "pacifies the brain" and "puts it to sleep." (Have you ever noticed how you can be completely mesmerized in front of the TV while "surfing" the cable channels? You keep channel surfing even though you're not really looking for anything.) Unlike productive activities like listening to storytelling or imaginative play, which create imagery, television "demands no output of energy from the brain." Could 6,000 hours of TV viewing in the first five years of life create a nation of children with sleeping brains? It's a chilling thought!

I believe it's time for parents to turn off the television. Replace television with family conversation, story reading, and storytelling (Pearce, 1992). Turn off the television when it's time to do homework. Turn it off so that kids can play. Play develops intelligence; watching television puts the brain to sleep.

2. Vote for smaller schools.

In his book *Greater Expectations*, William Damon provides parents with many sensible suggestions on parenting and schooling. Among the most important is his pitch for smaller schools. Community schools make education a personal experience. They are places where children build lasting personal relationships with people who care about them. Community schools sustain local values (Damon, 1995). I agree with Damon that in small community schools kids are more likely to develop character, competence, and good habits than they are in large schools. Small community schools are like homes; large sprawling schools are like factories. Community schools have school spirit. They have personalized instruction. They are places where parents are more likely to get involved. Smaller community schools are better places for children to grow and learn.

3. Vote for fewer kids per classroom.

A reduced number of children in the classroom is a very good idea. If your child is in a first grade classroom with thirty-three other first graders, he or she is probably getting cheated out of part of his or her education. The kind of personalized education that young kids need is impossible to deliver when the number of kids in a classroom is too high. If you know of politicians who are in favor of solving education funding problems by increasing class size, vote against them!

4. Make a big deal about good teachers.

Most people remember a teacher or two who really changed their lives. Teachers can have an incredible impact on helping kids find their purpose in life. Find ways to honor and support the teachers who are guiding your child and promoting his or her learning. Make sure teachers know you appreciate them. Good teachers are the key to better schools. They are much more important than technology, buildings, curriculum guides, tests, and reform movements. Don't be fooled by politicians—good teachers are more important than computers.

5. Pay attention.

Pay close attention to your child. Listen carefully, respond honestly, watch attentively. Check homework. Call out spelling words. Read a story. Find out what your child is writing about. Discuss the book he or she is reading. Describe your day at work and ask your child to tell you about things that are important to him or her. When parents pay attention, children learn to trust and share feelings.

If you are interested in the topics discussed in this chapter, here are some good books for further reading:

Damon, William. 1995. *Greater Expectations: Overcoming the Culture of Indulgence in America's Homes and School.* New York: The Free Press.

Kohn, Alfie. 1993. *Punished by Rewards: The Trouble with Gold Stars, Incentive Plans, A's, Praise, and Other Bribes.* Boston: Houghton Mifflin Company.

Pearce, Joseph Chilton. 1992. *Evolution's End: Claiming the Potential of Our Intelligence.* San Francisco: Harper San Francisco.

Sanders, Barry. 1994. *A is for Ox: The Collapse of Literacy and the Rise of Violence in an Electronic Age.* New York: Vintage Books.

Appendix A

Spelling Rules

Memorizing lots of spelling rules is old-fashioned. It doesn't work well because spelling rules are usually complicated and frightening like this one from Noah Webster's 1829 *Elementary Spelling Book:*

Formation of the plural number of nouns.

The regular plural of nouns is formed by the addition of *s* to the singular, which letter unites with most consonants in the same syllable, but sounds like *z* after all the consonants except *f, p, q, t, k,* or *c* with the sound of *k*.

Help your child learn a few good spelling rules. Here are some good rules with rough indicators of when your child may be ready for them:

Rule 1. The Qu Rule
Remember *Q* is always followed by *u*.
Exception: Iraq.
(Most spellers are ready for this Rule 1 in grade one.)

Rule 2. The Syllable Rule
Every syllable has a vowel or *y*.
(Rule 2 is developmentally appropriate by the middle or end of grade one.)

Rule 3. The Silent E Rule

When words end in silent *e*,

> drop the *e* when adding endings beginning with a vowel. (have, having)
> keep the *e* when adding endings beginning with a consonant. (late, lately)

(Rule 3 is developmentally appropriate around grade two.)

Rule 4. Changing Y to I

When the singular form ends with consonant + *y,* change the *y* to i and add *es.* (baby, babies.)

When the singular form ends with vowel + *y,* add *s.* (boy, boys)

(Rule 4 is developmentally appropriate around grades three and four.)

Rule 5. The IE or EI Rule:

Write *i* before *e*
Except after *c*
Or when sounded like *a*
As in neighbor and weigh.

Weird and neither
Aren't the same either.

Exceptions: caffeine, codeine, either, Fahrenheit, fiery, financier, height, hierarchy, leisure, neither, protein, seize, seizure, sheik, sleigh, stein, their, weird.

(Rule 5 is developmentally appropriate around grades four or five.)

B

Appendix B

Spelling Strategies to Use at Home

Here are five spelling strategies recommended for home use.

1. Visualizing Words.

When your child is writing and asks for a spelling, don't just spell the word out loud. Encourage your child to visualize the word. Follow the steps below to help your child store and retrieve the words visually. Remember, expert spellers see words in their mind's eye.

Visualizing Words

Step 1. Write the words on a card or scratch piece of paper.

Step 2. Have your child look at the word and remember the letter sequence visually.

Step 3. Remove the card and ask your child to try to "see" the word in his or her mind's eye.

Step 4. Have your child write the word from visual memory.

Step 5. Check for correct spelling.

2. Have-A-Go.

Children often know which words are misspelled in the first draft of a piece of their writing. Have-A-Go develops two good spelling habits: trying alternative spellings, and hunting down correct spellings. Here are instructions for your child:

Step 1. Circle three words you think you have misspelled in a piece of your writing.

Step 2. Get ready to Have-A-Go at spelling each word again. First you must concentrate. Shut your eyes and try to see how you think the word looks, or ask yourself if the meaning of the word gives you a clue to the correct spelling. Now you are ready to Have-A-Go. Write the word. Does it look right? If not, Have-A-Go again.

Step 3. Hunt down the correct spelling of each word. Check your Have-A-Go spelling. You may ask someone, look the spelling up, use a computer, or ask your parent to help you find the correct spelling.

3. Flip Folder.

Flip folder is a variation of Ernest Horn's tried-and-true technique in use as far back as 1919. Here's an updated version of the famous look-say-cover-write-check technique with instructions for your child:

Make two cuts on the front of a standard manila folder to create three flaps.

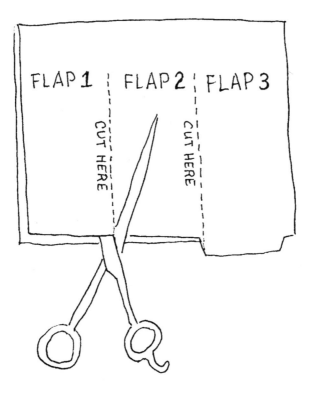

Write words to be studied in a column on a separate sheet of paper. Insert the sheet into the flip folder hiding the words to be studied under Flap 1.

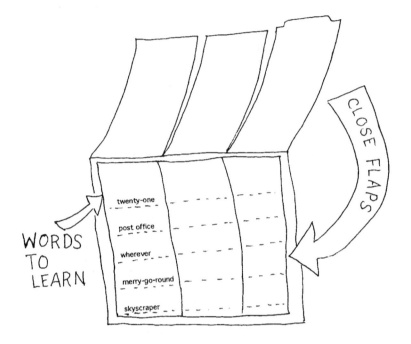

Now you are ready to look, say, see, write, and check.

Open Flap 1	**Look**	at the first word.
	Say	the first word.
Close all flaps	**See**	or visualize the word in your mind's eye
Open Flap 2	**Write**	the word in the center column.
Open Flaps 1 & 2	**Check**	your spelling.
Open Flap 3	**Rewrite**	the word in the third column from memory.

4. Spelling Games.

Popular words games like Scrabble, crossword puzzles, and hangman are good for developing word knowledge and spelling consciousness. Here's a sample word game called Word Scaffolds.

Word Scaffolds help children visualize spellings by relating letter strings in words with similar spelling patterns. This practice helps children acquire spelling by generalization which works more efficiently than the tedious memorization of too many elaborate spelling rules.

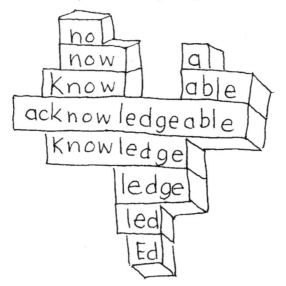

5. Finding and Learning Spelling Demons.

Kids need their own personal paperback dictionaries. Whenever they look up a word for spelling, they should put a dot beside the word. If they look up a word and find four dots beside it, they have identified one of their personal spelling demons—a word they use a lot but cannot remember how to spell.

Use creative associations called mnemonic devices to remember spellings for personal spelling demons. Here are some examples:

MNEMONICS—MEMORY DEVICES

all right	Two words. Associate with *all wrong*.
friend	*Fri*day is the *end* of the week.
hear	I h*ear* with my *ear*.
there	Is it *here* or t*here*?
potatoes	Pota*toes* have eyes and *toes*.
separate	There is *a rat* in sep*arat*e.
together	to+get+her
desert	*S*ahara (one *s*)
dessert	*s*omething *s*weet (two *s*'s) Which is fatter? The one you eat.
arithmetic	*A* rat *in* *T*om's *h*ouse *m*ight *e*at *T*om's *ice cream*.